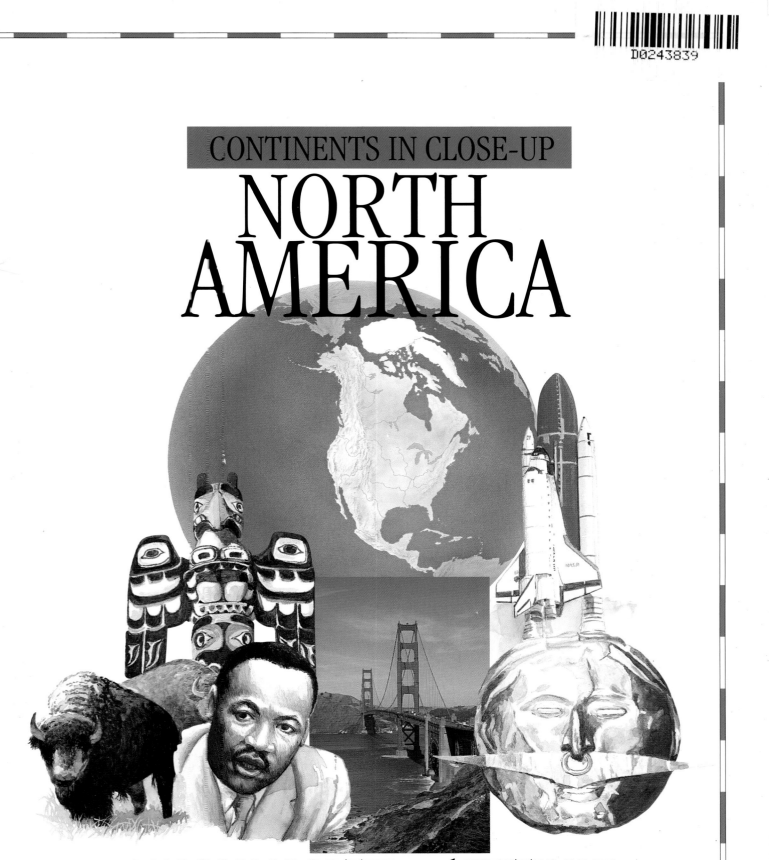

CONTINENTS IN CLOSE-UP
NORTH AMERICA

MALCOLM PORTER and KEITH LYE

CHERRYTREE BOOKS

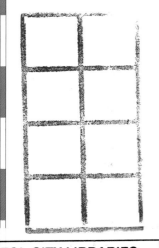
A Cherrytree Book

Designed and produced by
A S Publishing
Text by Keith Lye
Illustrated by Malcolm Porter and Raymond Turvey

New edition published 2008 by
Cherrytree Books, part of the
Evans Publishing Group
2a Portman Mansions
Chiltern Street
London W1U 6NR

Copyright © Malcolm Porter and AS Publishing

British Library Cataloguing in Publication data

Porter, Malcolm
    North America. - (continents in close-up)
    1.Children's atlases
    2.North America - Maps for children
    I.Title II.Lye, Keith
    912.7

ISBN 978 1842344583

Printed in Spain by Grafo SA

CONTINENTS IN CLOSE-UP
NORTH AMERICA

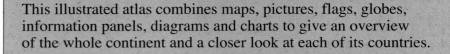

This illustrated atlas combines maps, pictures, flags, globes,
information panels, diagrams and charts to give an overview
of the whole continent and a closer look at each of its countries.

COUNTRY CLOSE-UPS

Each double-page spread has these
features:

Introduction The author introduces the
most important facts about the country
or region.

Globes A globe on which you can see the
country's position in the continent and the
world.

Flags Every country's flag is shown.

Information panels Every country has
an information panel which gives its area,
population and capital, and where possible
its other main towns, languages, religions,
government and currency.

Pictures Important features of each
country are illustrated and captioned to
give a flavour of the country. You can
find out about physical features, famous
people, ordinary people, animals, plants,
places, products and much more.

Maps Every country is shown on a
clear, accurate map. To get the most from
the maps it helps to know the symbols
which are shown in the key on the
opposite page.

Land You can see by the colouring on
the map where the land is forested,
frozen or desert.

Height Relief hill shading shows where
the mountain ranges are. Individual
mountains are marked by a triangle.

Direction All of the maps are drawn
with north at the top of the page.

Scale All of the maps are drawn to scale
so that you can find the distance
betweeen places in miles or kilometres.

0		200 miles
0		200 kilometres

KEY TO MAPS

CANADA	Country name
TEXAS	Province or state name
⌒	Country border
▪	More than 1 million people*
•	More than 500 000 people
·	Less than 500,000 people
☐	Country capital
★	State or province capital
ROCKY MTS	Mountain range
▲ Mt McKinley 6194m	Mountain with its height
∴ Tikal	Archaeological site

Ohio	River
⊢⊢⊢	Canal
⬭	Lake
⊢⊤	Dam
⬭	Island

	Forest
	Crops
	Dry grassland
	Desert
	Tundra
	Polar

Population figures in all cases are estimates, based on the most recent censuses where available or a variety of other sources.

CONTINENT CLOSE-UPS

People and Beliefs Map of population densities; chart of percentage of population per country; chart of areas of countries; map of religions; chart of main religious groups.

Climate and Vegetation Map of vegetation from polar to desert; map of winter and summer temperatures; map of annual rainfall; diagram of mountain climates.

Ecology and Environment Map of environmental problems and disasters; map of earthquake zones, volcanoes, hurricanes and tornadoes; diagram on greenhouse effect; panel on endangered animals and plants.

Economy Map of agricultural and industrial products; chart of gross domestic products for individual countries; panel on per capita gross domestic products; map of sources of energy.

Politics and History Map of political systems; panel of great events; timeline of important dates; panel showing Viking longboat and Voyager space probe; map of location of major events in North American history.

Index All the names on the maps and in the picture captions can be found in the index at the end of the book.

CONTENTS

Armadillo
see page 18

NORTH AMERICA

North America is the third largest continent after Asia and Africa. The two biggest countries, Canada and the United States, are among the world's richest. These two high-income countries have many high-tech industries and most people enjoy comfortable lives. Mexico and the countries of Central America and the Caribbean are low- or middle-income countries. Many of their people are poor.

The climate of North America varies greatly from north to south. A huge ice sheet covers most of Greenland in the northeast, with smaller ice caps in northern Canada. The southern parts of North America lie in the hot and humid tropics.

ALASKA (US)

PACIFIC OCEAN

Whales swim off the west coast of North America and people enjoy watching them. Many North Americans believe that the development of the land and sea should be controlled so that wildlife and natural wonders can be conserved.

Golden Gate Bridge in San Francisco, California, is one of North America's most famous landmarks. San Francisco was rebuilt after a great earthquake in 1906. Earthquakes and volcanic eruptions occur in western North America and in the Caribbean.

Market days, where farmers sell their produce and buy goods for their families, are important events in Central America. Farming employs more than 30 per cent of the people of tropical North America. Many farmers are poor and struggle to survive.

Combine harvesters are used on the huge cereal farms of Canada and the United States. Farming is highly mechanized here and employs only two per cent of the people. The farms are, however, much more productive than those in the countries to the south.

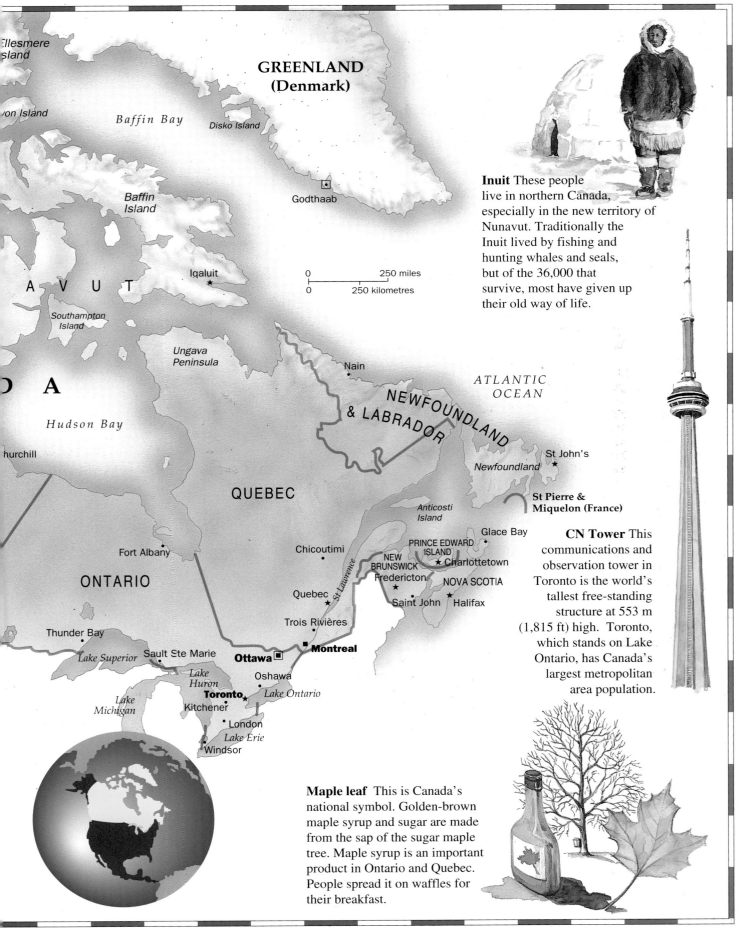

GREENLAND
(Denmark)

Baffin Bay

Disko Island

Ellesmere Island

on Island

Baffin Island

Godthaab

Southampton Island

Iqaluit

Ungava Peninsula

A V U T

Nain

Hudson Bay

ATLANTIC OCEAN

hurchill

NEWFOUNDLAND & LABRADOR

St John's

Newfoundland

St Pierre & Miquelon (France)

QUEBEC

Anticosti Island

Glace Bay

PRINCE EDWARD ISLAND

Chicoutimi

NEW BRUNSWICK

Charlottetown

Fort Albany

Fredericton

NOVA SCOTIA

ONTARIO

Quebec

St Laurence

Saint John

Halifax

Trois Rivières

Thunder Bay

Montreal

Lake Superior

Sault Ste Marie

Ottawa

Lake Huron

Oshawa

Toronto

Lake Ontario

Lake Michigan

Kitchener

London

Lake Erie

Windsor

0   250 miles
0   250 kilometres

Inuit These people live in northern Canada, especially in the new territory of Nunavut. Traditionally the Inuit lived by fishing and hunting whales and seals, but of the 36,000 that survive, most have given up their old way of life.

CN Tower This communications and observation tower in Toronto is the world's tallest free-standing structure at 553 m (1,815 ft) high. Toronto, which stands on Lake Ontario, has Canada's largest metropolitan area population.

Maple leaf This is Canada's national symbol. Golden-brown maple syrup and sugar are made from the sap of the sugar maple tree. Maple syrup is an important product in Ontario and Quebec. People spread it on waffles for their breakfast.

EASTERN CANADA

The four Atlantic provinces, together with Ontario and Quebec, make up eastern Canada. This region covers less than a third of Canada, but it contains about 70 per cent of the country's population. The most densely populated area extends along the shores of lakes Erie and Ontario and through the St Lawrence River valley. The river itself, together with several lakes, canals and locks, form a major waterway called the St Lawrence Seaway. This waterway is the outlet for the entire Great Lakes region.

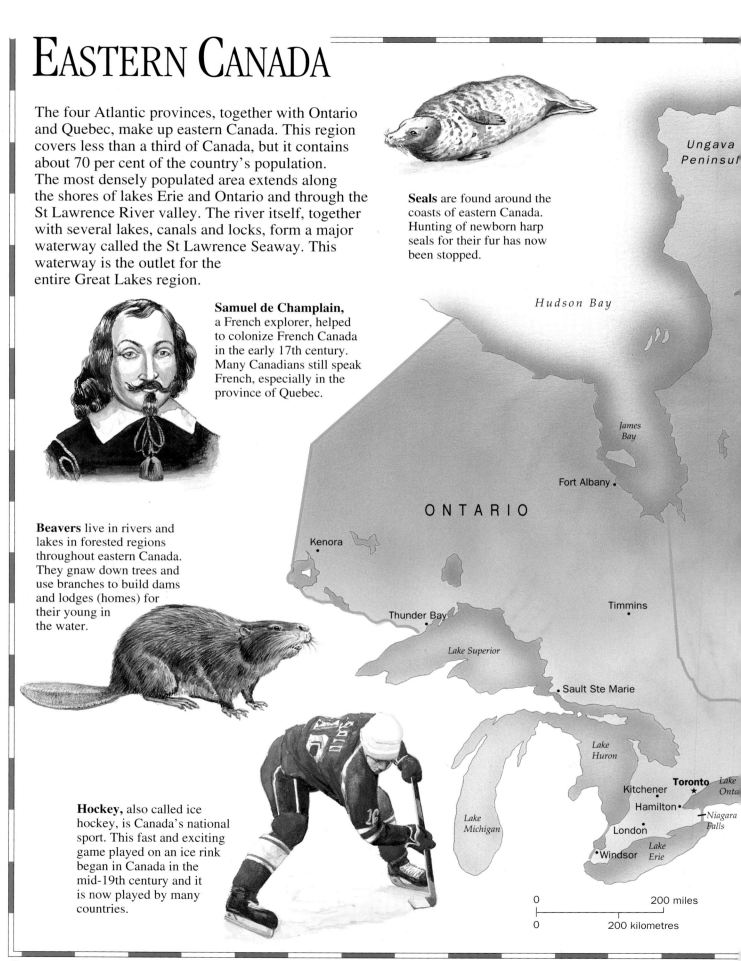

Seals are found around the coasts of eastern Canada. Hunting of newborn harp seals for their fur has now been stopped.

Samuel de Champlain, a French explorer, helped to colonize French Canada in the early 17th century. Many Canadians still speak French, especially in the province of Quebec.

Beavers live in rivers and lakes in forested regions throughout eastern Canada. They gnaw down trees and use branches to build dams and lodges (homes) for their young in the water.

Hockey, also called ice hockey, is Canada's national sport. This fast and exciting game played on an ice rink began in Canada in the mid-19th century and it is now played by many countries.

Ungava Peninsul

Hudson Bay

James Bay

Fort Albany

ONTARIO

Kenora

Timmins

Thunder Bay

Lake Superior

Sault Ste Marie

Lake Huron

Toronto
Kitchener
Hamilton
London
Windsor

Lake Michigan

Lake Erie

Lake Onta

Niagara Falls

| 0 | | 200 miles |
| 0 | | 200 kilometres |

UNITED STATES

Area: 9,529,063sq km (3,679,192sq miles)
Highest point: Mount McKinley, 6,194m (20,320ft)
Population: 298,444,000

Capital: Washington DC (pop 554,000)
Largest cities: New York City (8,104,000)
Los Angeles (3,846,000)
Chicago (2,862,000)
Official language: None (English is the chief language spoken in the United States, followed by Spanish)
Religions: Christianity (Protestant 52%, Roman Catholic 24%, others 6%), Mormon 2%, Judaism 1%, Islam 1%
Government: Federal republic
Currency: United States dollar

Bald eagle This majestic bird of prey was adopted as the national bird in 1782. Overhunting, pollution and the destruction of wilderness areas threatened its survival, but it is now protected.

New York City The country's largest city has a magnificent skyline. The '9/11' attack on the World Trade Centre, in which thousands lost their lives, destroyed the twin towers (top right).

Baseball is so popular that it has been called the national pastime of the United States. It was first played in the mid-18th century.

Exploring space Astronauts first landed on the moon in a lunar module like this in 1969. The United States is now using probes to explore Mars and the rest of the solar system.

MINNESOTA
St Paul ★
Lake Superior
MICHIGAN
Lake Huron
WISCONSIN
Lake Michigan
Madison ★   **Milwaukee** ■
Lansing ★   **Detroit** ★
Lake Erie
IOWA
Des Moines ★
Chicago ■
ILLINOIS
Springfield ★
INDIANA
Indianapolis ★
OHIO
Columbus ★
Cincinnati ■
Lake Ontario
Albany ★
NEW YORK
★ New York City
PENNSYLVANIA
Harrisburg ★
★ Trenton
Philadelphia ■
NEW JERSEY
Dover ★
DELAWARE
Washington DC ▣
Annapolis ★
MARYLAND
WEST VIRGINIA
Charleston ★
VIRGINIA
Richmond ★
Ohio
★ Frankfort
KENTUCKY
Nashville ★
Tennessee
Raleigh ★
NORTH CAROLINA
Appalachian Mts
Columbia ★
SOUTH CAROLINA
Mississippi
Kansas City ■
Topeka ★
KANSAS
Jefferson City ★
MISSOURI
St Louis ■
OKLAHOMA
Oklahoma City ★
Little Rock ★
ARKANSAS
TENNESSEE
ALABAMA
Montgomery ★
Atlanta ★
GEORGIA
MISSISSIPPI
Jackson ★
★ Tallahassee
Red
Dallas ■
Austin ★
Houston ■
LOUISIANA
Baton Rouge ★
■ **New Orleans**
FLORIDA
San Antonio ★
atte
Lincoln ★
Gulf of Mexico
● Miami
MAINE
Augusta ★
Montpelier ★
NEW HAMPSHIRE
VERMONT   ★ Concord
★ **Boston**
MASS.
Hartford ★   Providence ★
CONN.   R.I.
ATLANTIC OCEAN

13

NORTHEASTERN STATES

The northeastern states region includes the six New England states of Connecticut, Maine, Massachusetts, New Hampshire, Rhode Island and Vermont. It also includes Delaware, Maryland, New Jersey, New York and Pennsylvania. The map also shows the country's capital, Washington, which lies within an area called the District of Columbia. The Northeast contains fertile farmland, great industrial cities and many historic sites.

New England is a historic region that formed part of the original 13 British colonies which became the nucleus for the United States after the Revolutionary War of 1775-83. In the autumn New England's forests are ablaze with colour.

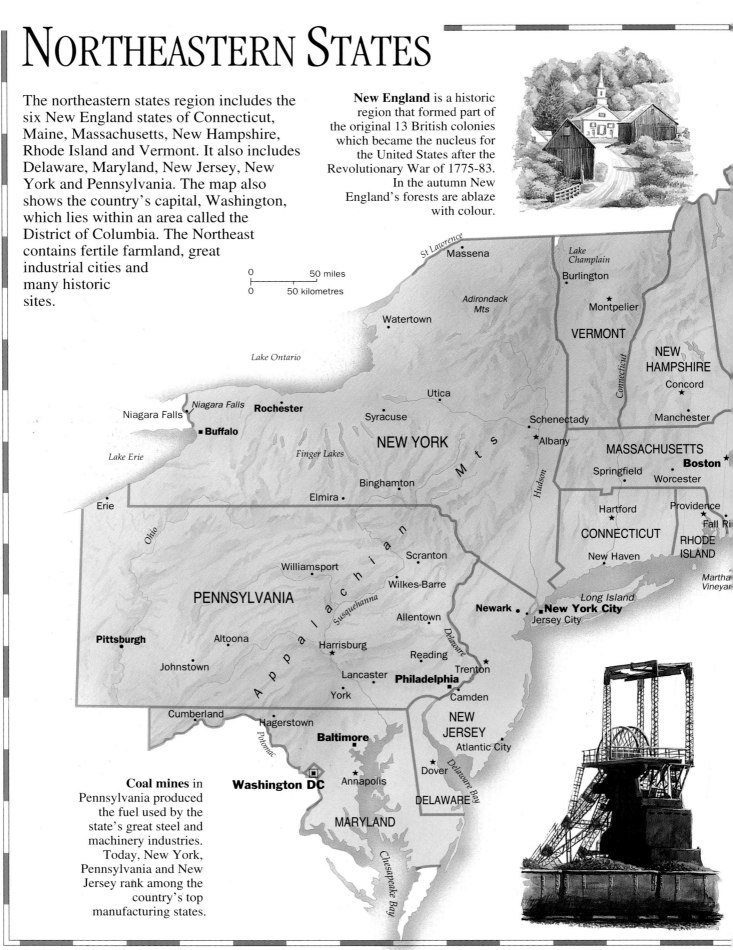

Coal mines in Pennsylvania produced the fuel used by the state's great steel and machinery industries. Today, New York, Pennsylvania and New Jersey rank among the country's top manufacturing states.

0 _____ 50 miles
0 _____ 50 kilometres

St Lawrence · Massena · Lake Champlain · Burlington

Adirondack Mts · Watertown · VERMONT · Montpelier · NEW HAMPSHIRE · Concord

Lake Ontario · Utica · Schenectady · Manchester

Niagara Falls · Rochester · Syracuse · Albany · MASSACHUSETTS

Niagara Falls · Buffalo · NEW YORK · Springfield · Boston · Worcester

Lake Erie · Finger Lakes · Hartford · Providence · Fall Ri

Binghamton · CONNECTICUT · RHODE ISLAND

Erie · Elmira · New Haven · Martha Vineyar

Ohio · Scranton · Long Island

Williamsport · Wilkes-Barre · Newark · New York City · Jersey City

PENNSYLVANIA · Allentown · Appalachian Mts · Susquehanna · Hudson · Connecticut

Pittsburgh · Altoona · Harrisburg · Reading · Trenton · Delaware

Johnstown · Lancaster · Philadelphia · Camden

York · NEW JERSEY

Cumberland · Hagerstown · Atlantic City

Potomac · Baltimore · Dover · Delaware Bay

Washington DC · Annapolis · DELAWARE

MARYLAND · Chesapeake Bay

Presque Isle

Moosehead Lake

MAINE

Bangor

Augusta ★

ATLANTIC OCEAN

Portland

Cape Cod

Nantucket Island

Capitol This is the building in Washington DC where Congress (the Senate and the House of Representatives) meets. President George Washington laid its cornerstone in 1793 and Congress first met there in 1800.

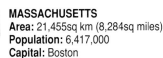

Covered bridges have a roof and sides that protect the wooden structure from the weather. The first long covered bridge in the United States was built in Massachusetts in 1806.

Liberty Bell This church bell in Philadelphia is a symbol of American freedom. It was rung on July 8, 1776, to announce the adoption of the Declaration of Independence. The bell broke in 1835 and is no longer rung.

Abraham Lincoln served as president of the United States between 1860 and 1865, when he was assassinated. He led the nation during the Civil War (1861-65).

CONNECTICUT
Area: 12,997sq km (5,018sq miles)
Population: 3,504,000
Capital: Hartford

DELAWARE
Area: 5,294sq km (2,045sq miles)
Population: 830,000
Capital: Dover

MAINE
Area: 86,156sq km (33,265sq miles)
Population: 1,317,000
Capital: Augusta

MARYLAND
Area: 27,091sq km (10,460sq miles)
Population: 5,558,000
Capital: Annapolis

MASSACHUSETTS
Area: 21,455sq km (8,284sq miles)
Population: 6,417,000
Capital: Boston

NEW HAMPSHIRE
Area: 24,032sq km (9,279sq miles)
Population: 1,300,000
Capital: Concord

NEW JERSEY
Area: 20,168sq km (7,787sq miles)
Population: 8,699,000
Capital: Trenton

NEW YORK
Area: 136,583sq km (52,735sq miles)
Population: 19,227,000
Capital: Albany

PENNSYLVANIA
Area: 119,251sq km (46,043sq miles)
Population: 12,408,000
Capital: Harrisburg

RHODE ISLAND
Area: 3,139sq km (1,212sq miles)
Population: 1,081,000
Capital: Providence

VERMONT
Area: 24,900sq km (9,614sq miles)
Population: 621,000
Capital: Montpelier

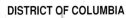
DISTRICT OF COLUMBIA
Area: 179sq km (69sq miles)
Population: 554,000

SOUTHEASTERN STATES

The southeastern states contain large areas of coastal plains and the southern part of the scenic Appalachian Mountains. The region is rich in history. Virginia, North and South Carolina and Georgia were among the 13 English colonies that formed the nucleus of the United States, while the region also played a major part in the Civil War. The states once depended on farming, but manufacturing is now important.

Coca-Cola is regarded as a symbol of American taste all over the world. It was first produced by a pharmacist, John S. Pemberton, in Atlanta in 1886. The Coca-Cola Company, founded in 1892, keeps secret the ingredients used in the drink.

Louisville Frankfor
Lexing
Ohio
KENTUCKY

Cumberland
Nashville Knoxvil
TENNESSEE
Memphis Chattanooga

Tennessee

Birmingham **Atlan**

ALABAMA
Colum

Montgomery

Alabama

Mobile

Pensacola Tallahassee

Gulf of Mexico

Stone Mountain This granite mountain near Atlanta, Georgia, has a huge sculpture carved on it as a memorial to the heroes of the South in the Civil War. The sculpture shows Jefferson Davis, Robert E. Lee and Stonewall Jackson.

Martin Luther King Jr. was the main leader of the Civil Rights movement in the 1950s and 1960s. His demands for justice for African Americans brought him worldwide fame. He was assassinated in 1968.

American alligators were once common along the coasts of the Gulf of Mexico and the Atlantic coast as far north as South Carolina. But so many were hunted and killed that they became scarce. Today they are protected in many areas.

Cotton was the chief crop of the southeastern states in the 19th century. Before the Civil War, it was picked by slaves. Today the region also produces several warm-weather crops, such as sugar cane, rice and tobacco.

Map labels

Parkersburg
WEST VIRGINIA
★ Charleston
Arlington
Shenandoah
Charlottesville
VIRGINIA
Richmond ★
Lynchburg
James
Norfolk
• Virginia Beach
Chesapeake Bay

Greensboro
NORTH CAROLINA ★ Raleigh
Charlotte
Pee Dee
Fayetteville
Cape Hatteras
Rock Hill
Columbia
★
Florence
• Jacksonville
• Wilmington

ATLANTIC
OCEAN

SOUTH CAROLINA
Augusta
Savannah
• Charleston
Macon
GEORGIA
Savannah
Altamaha

Jacksonville
• Gainesville
FLORIDA
Daytona Beach
Orlando
Cape Canaveral
Tampa
St Petersburg
Lake Okeechobee
Fort Myers
Everglades
Fort Lauderdale
■ Miami
Key West • *Florida Keys*

Popular music
American music has
influenced musicians
throughout the world.
Popular musical forms
in the 20th century
include gospel, jazz,
country and western,
rhythm and blues,
rock'n'roll and rap.

ALABAMA
Area: 133,915sq km (51,705sq miles)
Population: 4,530,000
Capital: Montgomery

FLORIDA
Area: 151,939sq km (58,664sq miles)
Population: 17,397,000
Capital: Tallahassee

GEORGIA
Area: 152,576sq km (58,910sq miles)
Population: 8,829,000
Capital: Atlanta

KENTUCKY
Area: 104,659sq km (40,410sq miles)
Population: 4,146,000
Capital: Frankfort

NORTH CAROLINA
Area: 136,412sq km (52,669sq miles)
Population: 8,542,000
Capital: Raleigh

SOUTH CAROLINA
Area: 80,582sq km (31,113sq miles)
Population: 4,198,000
Capital: Columbia

TENNESSEE
Area: 109,152sq km (42,144sq miles)
Population: 5,901,000
Capital: Nashville

VIRGINIA
Area: 105,586sq km (40,767sq miles)
Population: 7,460,000
Capital: Richmond

WEST VIRGINIA
Area: 62,758sq km (24,232sq miles)
Population: 1,815,000
Capital: Charleston

John F. Kennedy Space Center
This site at Cape Canaveral is
used by NASA for its manned
space flights. It is a major
tourist attraction in Florida, the
'Sunshine State'.

0   100 miles
0   100 kilometres

SOUTH-CENTRAL STATES

Arkansas, Louisiana and Mississippi, which form the eastern part of the south-central states, are drained by the Mississippi River valley. In the west lie the vast open spaces of Texas and Oklahoma. These two states, together with Louisiana, are among the top five petroleum producers in the United States. The region also contains some major cities, including Houston, San Antonio and Dallas, which are among the country's top ten cities.

Armadillos are burrowing animals found throughout the south-central and southeastern states. Their bony plates protect them from most predators, but many are killed by vehicles when they are crossing roads.

Texas longhorns These cattle were the forerunners of the beef cattle that today provide about half of the farm incomes of Texas. Cattle ranches cover huge areas of the state.

Alamo This former Roman Catholic mission in San Antonio, Texas, was besieged by a Mexican army between February 23 and March 6, 1836. The bravery of the Texan defenders inspired others to achieve Texan independence.

Seafoods, including shrimp, crabs, crayfish and oysters, are used in many dishes in the south-central states. Seafood is an ingredient in many spicy Louisiana dishes, such as gumbo.

North Canadian
Cimarron
Canadian
Amarillo
Oklahoma
OKLAHOM
Lubbock
Wichita Falls·
· El Paso
Abilene
·
Rio Grande
T E X A S
Pecos
San Angelo
Colorado
Aust
San Anton
Laredo
Corpus Chr
Browns·

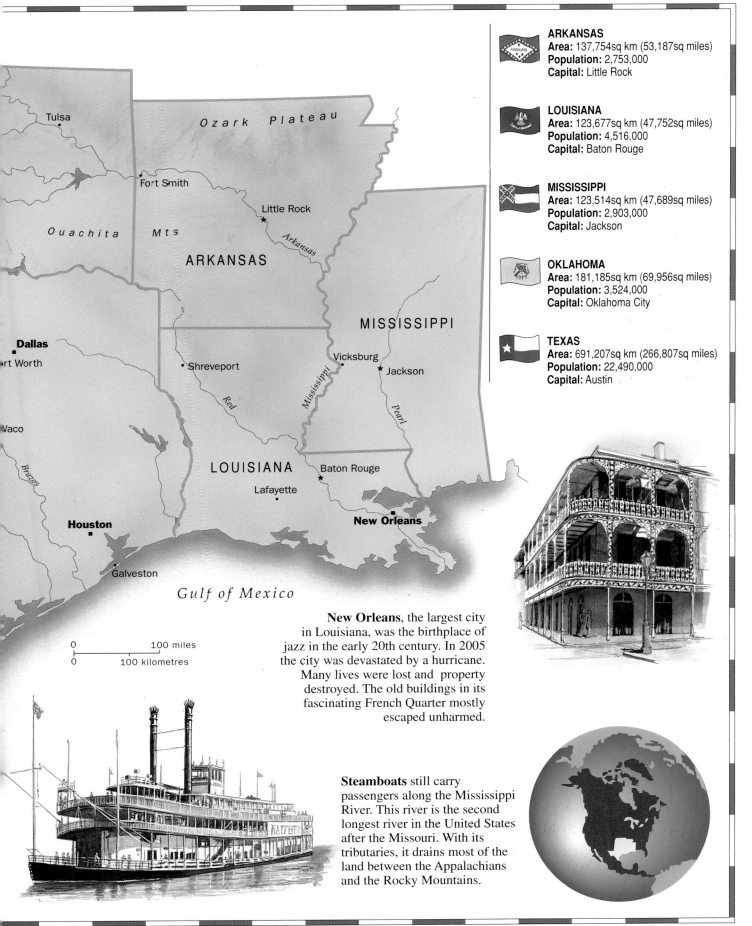

ARKANSAS
Area: 137,754sq km (53,187sq miles)
Population: 2,753,000
Capital: Little Rock

LOUISIANA
Area: 123,677sq km (47,752sq miles)
Population: 4,516,000
Capital: Baton Rouge

MISSISSIPPI
Area: 123,514sq km (47,689sq miles)
Population: 2,903,000
Capital: Jackson

OKLAHOMA
Area: 181,185sq km (69,956sq miles)
Population: 3,524,000
Capital: Oklahoma City

TEXAS
Area: 691,207sq km (266,807sq miles)
Population: 22,490,000
Capital: Austin

Tulsa

Ozark Plateau

Fort Smith

Ouachita Mts

Little Rock

Arkansas

ARKANSAS

MISSISSIPPI

Dallas

rt Worth

Shreveport

Vicksburg

Jackson

Waco

Red

Mississippi

Pearl

Brazos

LOUISIANA

Baton Rouge

Lafayette

Houston

New Orleans

Galveston

Gulf of Mexico

0   100 miles
0   100 kilometres

New Orleans, the largest city
in Louisiana, was the birthplace of
jazz in the early 20th century. In 2005
the city was devastated by a hurricane.
Many lives were lost and property
destroyed. The old buildings in its
fascinating French Quarter mostly
escaped unharmed.

Steamboats still carry
passengers along the Mississippi
River. This river is the second
longest river in the United States
after the Missouri. With its
tributaries, it drains most of the
land between the Appalachians
and the Rocky Mountains.

MIDWESTERN STATES

The 12 midwestern states cover about a fifth of the United States. The land is mostly flat, including parts of the Great Plains in the west and the lower Interior Plains south and west of the Great Lakes. Farmers produce grains and other crops on the fertile land, together with dairy products and livestock. Major industrial cities include Chicago, Detroit and Indianapolis. The Great Lakes and the Mississippi River are used to transport goods.

Bison once roamed the Midwest in huge herds, but hunters slaughtered most of them. Today a few thousand live in protected areas.

Mount Rushmore National Memorial, South Dakota, is a carving of four presidents: George Washington, Thomas Jefferson, Theodore Roosevelt and Abraham Lincoln. Each face is about 18m (60ft) high.

American football is played by university and college teams. The professional National Football League is divided into the American Football Conference and the National Football Conference.

Pioneers had reached the Mississippi by the 1820s. In the 1840s wagon trains crossed the Great Plains and, by the 1890s, scattered settlements had sprung up all across this dry region.

NORTH DAKOTA
Red Lake
Lake Sakakawea
Fargo
Duluth
★ Bismarck
MINNESOTA
Great Plains
Minneapolis • • ★ St Paul
Mississ
SOUTH DAKOTA
Black Hills
Pierre ★ Lake Oahe
Sioux Falls •
▲ Mt Rushmore
Missouri
Sioux City •
Cedar Rap
IOWA
★ Des Moines
NEBRASKA
Platte
Omaha •
Lincoln ★
Kansas
★ Kansas City
Topeka
Jefferson C ★
KANSAS
MISSOU
Wichita •

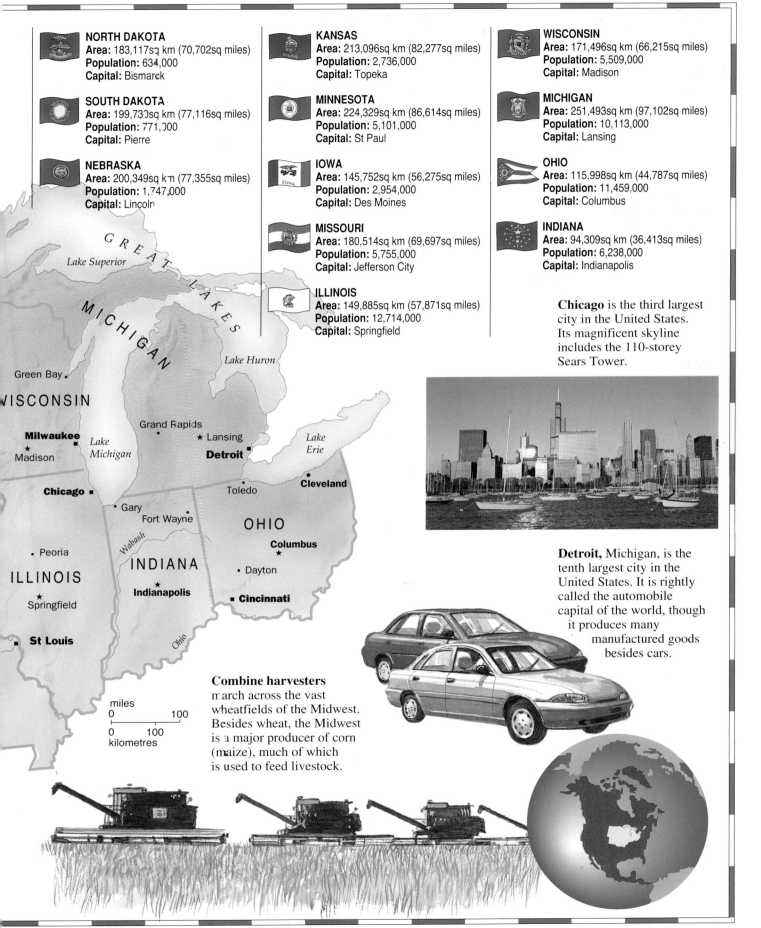

NORTH DAKOTA
Area: 183,117sq km (70,702sq miles)
Population: 634,000
Capital: Bismarck

SOUTH DAKOTA
Area: 199,730sq km (77,116sq miles)
Population: 771,000
Capital: Pierre

NEBRASKA
Area: 200,349sq km (77,355sq miles)
Population: 1,747,000
Capital: Lincoln

KANSAS
Area: 213,096sq km (82,277sq miles)
Population: 2,736,000
Capital: Topeka

MINNESOTA
Area: 224,329sq km (86,614sq miles)
Population: 5,101,000
Capital: St Paul

IOWA
Area: 145,752sq km (56,275sq miles)
Population: 2,954,000
Capital: Des Moines

MISSOURI
Area: 180,514sq km (69,697sq miles)
Population: 5,755,000
Capital: Jefferson City

ILLINOIS
Area: 149,885sq km (57,871sq miles)
Population: 12,714,000
Capital: Springfield

WISCONSIN
Area: 171,496sq km (66,215sq miles)
Population: 5,509,000
Capital: Madison

MICHIGAN
Area: 251,493sq km (97,102sq miles)
Population: 10,113,000
Capital: Lansing

OHIO
Area: 115,998sq km (44,787sq miles)
Population: 11,459,000
Capital: Columbus

INDIANA
Area: 94,309sq km (36,413sq miles)
Population: 6,238,000
Capital: Indianapolis

Chicago is the third largest city in the United States. Its magnificent skyline includes the 110-storey Sears Tower.

Detroit, Michigan, is the tenth largest city in the United States. It is rightly called the automobile capital of the world, though it produces many manufactured goods besides cars.

Combine harvesters march across the vast wheatfields of the Midwest. Besides wheat, the Midwest is a major producer of corn (maize), much of which is used to feed livestock.

NORTHWESTERN STATES

The eastern part of the northwestern states is part of the flat Great Plains. But the west is largely mountainous. The Cascade Range in Oregon and Washington has active volcanoes, including Mount Saint Helens, which exploded with great force in 1980, killing 57 people. Alaska, which became the 49th state on 3 January, 1959, also has active volcanoes. Alaska is rich in oil, while farming and forestry are important in the other five states.

Aircraft are made by the Boeing Company, which has its headquarters in Seattle. The city is also the home of Microsoft, the world's leading computer software company. The manufacture of wood products and processed foods are other major industries in the Northwest.

Mount McKinley, in south-central Alaska, is the highest mountain in North America. It got its name from William McKinley who was US President from 1897-1901. Its Native American name Denali means 'The Great One'.

Map labels

Bellingham
Bremerton • ■ Seattle
Spokane
Aberdeen •
Olympia ★ • Tacoma
WASHINGTON
Mt Rainier ▲
4392m   Yakima •
Mt St Helens
2950m ▲   Kennewick •   Walla Walla   Lewis
Portland ■   Columbia
PACIFIC OCEAN
Salem ★
Cascade Range
Blue Mts
Eugene •
• Bend
OREGON   Bois ★
Medford •   Great Basin   Namp
• Klamath Falls   Snake

Beaufort Sea
Barrow
Brooks Range
Bering Strait
• Nome
ALASKA
Yukon
Fairbanks •
Mt McKinley ▲
6194m   Range
Alaska
Anchorage •
Bering Sea
Seward •
Skagway
Juneau ★
PACIFIC OCEAN
Aleutian Islands

0 ———— 300 miles
0 ———— 300 kilometres

Grizzly bears roam the forests of Alaska and western Canada. Some also live in remote areas of the northwestern states, but many of the places where the bears once lived are now occupied by people.

ALASKA
Area: 1,530,693sq km (591,004sq miles)
Population: 655,000
Capital: Juneau

IDAHO
Area: 216,430sq km (83,564sq miles)
Population: 1,393,000
Capital: Boise

MONTANA
Area: 380,849sq km (147,046sq miles)
Population: 927,000
Capital: Helena

OREGON
Area: 251,418sq km (97,073sq miles)
Population: 3,595,000
Capital: Salem

WASHINGTON
Area: 176,479sq km (68,139sq miles)
Population: 6,204,000
Capital: Olympia

WYOMING
Area: 253,324sq km (97,809sq miles)
Population: 507,000
Capital: Cheyenne

Native Americans in the Northwest fished and hunted animals. They also gathered plant foods in the forests. They used wood to build houses and boats, and to make containers, bowls, utensils and masks like this one.

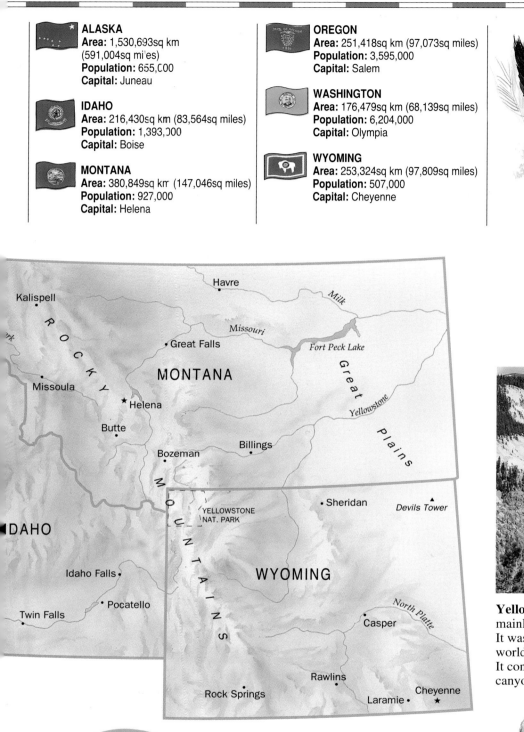

Kalispell · Havre · Milk · Missouri · Great Falls · Fort Peck Lake · ROCKY · MONTANA · Missoula · Helena ★ · Butte · Bozeman · Billings · Great Plains · Yellowstone · IDAHO · YELLOWSTONE NAT. PARK · Sheridan · ▲ Devils Tower · MOUNTAINS · WYOMING · Idaho Falls · Pocatello · Twin Falls · North Platte · Casper · Rock Springs · Rawlins · Cheyenne ★ · Laramie ·

Yellowstone National Park lies mainly in northwestern Wyoming. It was set up in 1872 and is the world's oldest national park. It contains hot springs and geysers, canyons and huge waterfalls.

0 — 100 miles
0 — 100 kilometres

Devils Tower, in northeastern Wyoming, is a mountain formed from hard volcanic rock. It rises 264m (865ft) from its base. It became the country's first national monument in 1906.

23

SOUTHWESTERN STATES

The southwestern states contain much magnificent scenery. California has more people than any other state and is the country's leading manufacturing and farming state. It also has valuable mineral deposits, including oil and natural gas. If California were a separate country, it would rank among the world's top ten in terms of the total value of the goods and services it produces. Hawaii, in the Pacific Ocean, became the 50th state on 21 August 1959.

Surfing is an exciting sport along the Pacific coast of California and also in Hawaii. The northern shores of Oahu, Hawaii, attract surfers from all over the world.

Silicon Valley is an area in California between San José and nearby Palo Alto that is home to the computer industry. Silicon is used to make the microprocessors in computers.

Deserts cover large areas in the Southwest. Some desert plants, such as cacti, have long, shallow roots that obtain every drop of moisture from a large area. Their swollen stems store water.

HAWAII

Kauai
Niihau
Oahu
★ Honolulu
Molokai
Lanai
Maui
Kahoolawe
Mauna Kea 4205m ▲
Mauna Loa 4169m ▲
Hawaii

| 0 | 100 miles |
| 0 | 100 kilometres |

PACIFIC OCEAN

Eureka •

Sacramento

Coastal

Chico •

Humboldt

Reno •
Carson City ★
Lake Tahoe

NEVADA

Great Basin

Sacramento ★

Oakland ■ • Stockton
San Francisco •
San José •

Sierra Nevada

Fresno •

Ranges

Death Valley

Las Vegas •
Lake Mead

CALIFORNIA

Santa Barbara •

Mojave Desert

San Bernardino •
Lake Havasu City

PACIFIC OCEAN

Los Angeles ■

Colorado

San Diego ■

Salton Sea

Yuma •

| 0 | 100 miles |
| 0 | 100 kilometres |

Kilauea is an active volcano on the eastern slope of Mauna Loa, Hawaii. It emits runny lava that flows down to the sea. All of the islands in Hawaii were formed by volcanoes. But only the volcanoes on Hawaii itself are active. The others are extinct.

Grand Canyon This huge canyon was worn out by the Colorado River and is around 1.6km (1 mile) deep in places. The canyon, like many of the country's scenic wonders, is protected in a national park.

 ARIZONA
Area: 295,259sq km (114,000sq miles)
Population: 5,744,000
Capital: Phoenix

CALIFORNIA
Area: 411,047sq km (158,706sq miles)
Population: 35,894,000
Capital: Sacramento

COLORADO
Area: 269,594sq km (104,091sq miles)
Population: 4,601,000
Capital: Denver

HAWAII
Area: 16,760sq km (6,471sq miles)
Population: 1,263,000
Capital: Honolulu

NEVADA
Area: 286,352sq km (110,561sq miles)
Population: 2,335,000
Capital: Carson City

NEW MEXICO
Area: 314,924sq km (121,593sq miles)
Population: 1,903,000
Capital: Santa Fe

UTAH
Area: 219,887sq km (84,899sq miles)
Population: 2,389,000
Capital: Salt Lake City

Mesa Verde is a national park in southwestern Colorado. Its name means 'green table' and it contains impressive remains of cliff dwellings built by Native Americans hundreds of years ago.

MEXICO

Mexico, the third largest country in North America, forms a bridge between the United States and the seven countries of Central America. The land is mainly mountainous, with deserts in the north and rainforests in the south. Temperatures vary according to the height of the land. Farming is important, but Mexico's main exports are oil and oil products. Factories in the north assemble goods, such as vehicle parts, for US companies.

MEXICO

Area: 1,972,547sq km (761,605sq miles)
Highest point: Citlaltépetl (also called Orizaba), 5,700m (18,701ft)
Population: 107,450,000
Capital and largest city: Mexico City (pop 18,660,000)
Other large cities: Guadalajara (3,697,000) Monterrey (3,267,000) Puebla (1,888,000)
Official language: Spanish
Religion: Christianity (Roman Catholic 89%, Protestant 5%, other 5%)
Government: Federal republic
Currency: Mexican peso

Tarantula is the popular name given to large hairy bird-eating spiders of the family Theraphosidae, which are found between the southwestern United States and South America. They look frightening but their bite is generally not serious.

Tijuana Mexicali Colorado

Ciudad Juárez

Hermosillo

Chihuahua

Baja California

Gulf of California

Sierra Madre Occidental

Culiacán

Dura

La Paz

Mazatlán

PACIFIC OCEAN

T

Monarch butterfly This colourful creature holds the record among insects for the distance it migrates each year. In autumn, it travels from New England to the southern United States and Mexico. In spring it returns to the north.

Acapulco is Mexico's leading Pacific Ocean resort. Tourism is a major industry in Mexico. Some people come to the seaside resorts while others want to see the great Native American historic sites.

Gold and silver objects made by Aztecs are evidence of their artistic skills. According to legend, the Aztec capital, Tenochtitlán, was founded in 1325. The Aztecs were defeated by Spanish soldiers in 1521.

Oil is produced along the southeastern coasts of the Gulf of Mexico and also offshore. Mexico has exported oil since the 1970s. The country also produces silver and other metals.

Mayan pyramids in southern Mexico are reminders of the great Native American civilization that flourished between AD 250 and 900. The Mayan empire extended from Mexico, through Guatemala and Belize into El Salvador and Honduras.

Mexico City became one of the world's fastest growing cities in the late 20th century and is now one of the world's largest urban areas. It stands on a high plateau and was the site of the Aztec capital, Tenochtitlán.

Rio Grande

Rio Bravo del Norte

Nuevo Laredo

Sierra Madre Oriental

Monterrey

Reynosa

• **Torreón**

Saltillo

Matamoros

MEXICO

• Tampico

• Aguascalientes

Guadalajara

Morelia

Mexico City

Colima

Balsas

Cuernavaca

Puebla

Jalapa

• **Veracruz**

Citlaltépetl (Orizaba) 5700m

Sierra Madre del Sur

Oaxaca

Villahermosa

Acapulco

Tapachula •

Gulf of Mexico

Cancún

Mérida

Chichén Itzá

Yucatán Peninsula

Campeche

Ciudad del Carmen

0   200 miles

0   200 kilometres

WESTERN CENTRAL AMERICA

Western Central America consists of four countries: Belize, El Salvador, Guatemala and Honduras. Hot and humid coasts border the region in the north and south. Between lies a highland zone with many active volcanoes. The people include Native Americans, together with people of African and European descent. Many people are of mixed origin. Farming is the main activity. Most people live in the cooler highlands.

Coral reefs and islands stretch along the swampy coast of Belize. They form the world's second longest barrier reef after Australia's Great Barrier Reef and they are an important breeding area for fish.

BELIZE

Area: 22,965sq km (8,867sq miles)
Population: 287,000
Capital: Belmopan (pop 9,000)
Largest city: Belize City (50,000)
Government: Constitutional monarchy
Official language: English
Currency: Belize dollar

EL SALVADOR

Area: 21,041sq km (8,124 sq miles)
Population: 6,822,000
Capital and largest city: San Salvador (pop 1,424,000)
Government: Republic
Official language: Spanish
Currency: US dollar

GUATEMALA

Area: 108,889sq km (42,042sq miles)
Population: 12,294,000
Capital and largest city: Guatemala City (pop 951,000)
Government: Republic
Official language: Spanish
Currency: Quetzal, US dollar

HONDURAS

Area: 112,088sq km (43,277sq miles)
Population: 7,326,000
Capital and largest city: Tegucigalpa (pop 1,007,000)
Government: Republic
Official language: Spanish
Currency: Lempira

Belize City
Tikal
Belmopan
BELIZE
0   50 miles
0   50 kilometres
Chixoy
Puerto Barrios
GUATEMALA
Lake Izabal
▲ Tajumulco 4210m
Motagua
Quezaltenango
Mazatenango
Guatemala City
Antigua
Santa Ana
San Salvador
PACIFIC OCEAN
Sonsonate
EL SALVADOR

Coffee is grown in the highlands of Central America and most of the berries on the coffee plants are hand picked. Coffee is the chief export of El Salvador, Guatemala and Honduras.

Tikal, in northern Guatemala, contains huge ruined pyramids. It was the biggest city of the Maya. Its main temple stood on top of a pyramid 45m (150ft) tall.

Bananas grow well in hot, wet climates and they are a leading crop on the lowlands of Central America. The other main crop grown for export in lowland areas is sugar cane.

Caribbean Sea

Gulf of Honduras

Islas de la Bahía

• Tela

• La Ceiba

n Pedro
Sula

Patuca

• Juticalpa

HONDURAS

Tegucigalpa

• Miguel

Manatees, or sea cows, live along the Caribbean coasts of Central America and northern South America. Found in sheltered coastal waters, they have suffered from the effects of pollution and the use of power boats.

Market days in Guatemalan towns and villages are lively occasions, when farmers bring their products for sale. About one-third of Guatemala's people are direct descendants of the original Native Americans.

EASTERN CENTRAL AMERICA

Like western Central America, Costa Rica, Nicaragua and Panama have hot, tropical climates except in highland areas which are cooler. Nicaragua is the largest country in Central America. Like Costa Rica, it lies in an unstable area where earthquakes and volcanic eruptions are common. Costa Rica has many beautiful national parks and now attracts many tourists. Panama is an isthmus, a narrow strip of land linking North and South America.

 **COSTA RICA**

Area: 50,700sq km (19,575sq miles)
Population: 4,075,000
Capital and largest city: San José (pop 1,085,000)
Government: Republic
Official language: Spanish
Religions: Christianity (Roman Catholic 76%)
Currency: Costa Rican colón

 **NICARAGUA**

Area: 130,000sq km (50,193sq miles)
Population: 5,570,000
Capital and largest city: Managua (pop 1,098,000)
Government: Republic
Official language: Spanish
Religions: Christianity (Roman Catholic 73%)
Currency: Córdoba

 **PANAMA**

Area: 77,082sq km (29,762sq miles)
Population: 3,191,000
Capital and largest city: Panama City (pop 930,000)
Government: Republic
Official language: Spanish
Religions: Christianity (Roman Catholic 85%)
Currency: Balboa

Pan-American Highway
This road system extends through the Americas from the United States border to southern Chile. The only break is in Panama where the route is blocked by dense rainforest.

Active volcanoes Volcanic eruptions are common throughout the highlands of Nicaragua and Costa Rica. The volcanic rocks have weathered to produce rich, fertile soils.

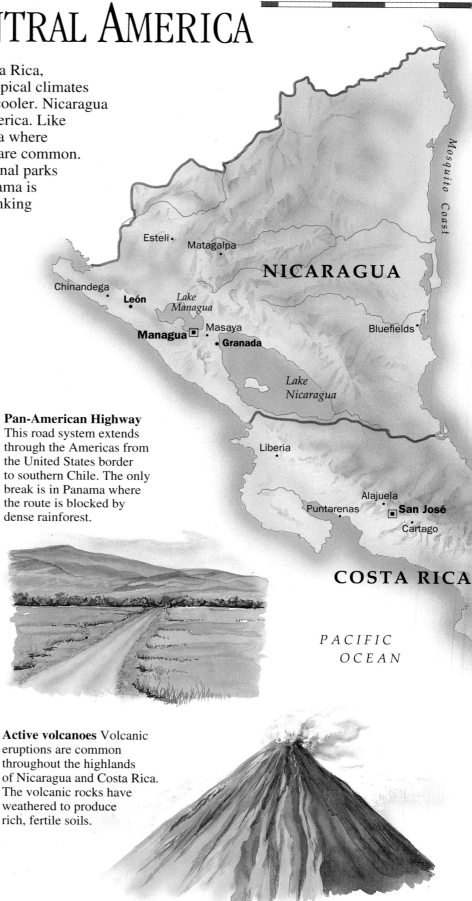

Mosquito Coast

Esteli
Matagalpa
NICARAGUA
Chinandega
León
Lake Managua
Masaya
Bluefields
Managua
Granada
Lake Nicaragua
Liberia
Alajuela
Puntarenas
San José
Cartago
COSTA RICA
PACIFIC OCEAN

Rainforests once covered most of the region. But large areas of forest have been cut down to create farmland, towns, factories and so on. The destruction of forests has caused a great loss of tropical plants and animals.

Emerald toucanets live in forests from southern Mexico to Peru. They are noisy birds but their green plumage makes them hard to see. Central America is rich in birdlife, with species from both North and South America.

Panama Canal This waterway links the Atlantic and Pacific oceans and saves ships from having to sail around South America. The Canal was completed in 1914. It is almost 82km (51 miles) long. A major project to expand it is due to be completed in 2014.

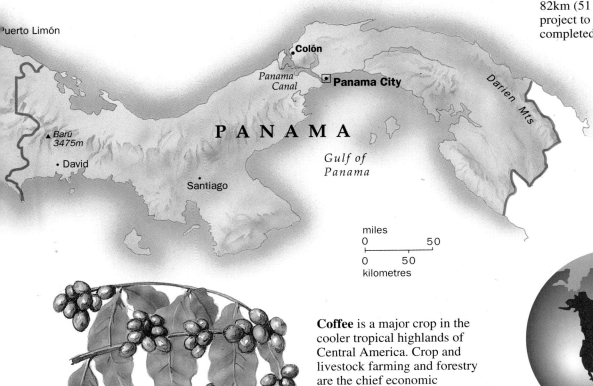

Caribbean Sea

Puerto Limón

• **Colón**

Panama Canal

⊡ **Panama City**

Darien Mts

P A N A M A

▲ *Barú 3475m*

• David

Gulf of Panama

• Santiago

miles
0   50

0   50
kilometres

Coffee is a major crop in the cooler tropical highlands of Central America. Crop and livestock farming and forestry are the chief economic activities in eastern Central America.

NORTHERN CARIBBEAN

The largest Caribbean island nations are Cuba, the Dominican Republic and Haiti, followed by the Bahamas and Jamaica. Puerto Rico is a US Commonwealth, while the Cayman Islands and the Turks and Caicos Islands are British overseas territories. Most people are descended from Europeans, and Africans who came to the Caribbean as slaves. Sugar and coffee are leading crops. Manufacturing, mining and tourism are also important.

Fidel Castro led revolutionary forces to power in Cuba in 1959. His Communist policies and his close ties with the Soviet Union, which was dissolved in 1991, were opposed by the United States.

BAHAMAS

Area: 13,935sq km (5,380sq miles)
Population: 304,000
Capital: Nassau (pop 222,000)
Currency: Bahamian dollar

CUBA

Area: 110,861sq km (42,804sq miles)
Population: 11,383,000
Capital: Havana (pop 2,189,000)
Currency: Cuban peso

DOMINICAN REPUBLIC

Area: 48,734sq km (18,816sq miles)
Population: 9,184,000
Capital: Santo Domingo (pop 1,865,000)
Currency: Dominican peso

HAITI

Area: 27,750sq km (10,714sq miles)
Population: 8,309,000
Capital: Port-au-Prince (pop 1,961,000)
Currency: Gourde

JAMAICA

Area: 10,991sq km (4,244sq miles)
Population: 2,758,000
Capital: Kingston (pop 575,000)
Currency: Jamaican dollar

OVERSEAS TERRITORIES

CAYMAN ISLANDS (UK)
Area: 259sq km (100sq miles)
Population: 45,000
Capital: George Town

PUERTO RICO (US)
Area: 8,897sq km (3,435sq miles)
Population: 3,927,000
Capital: San Juan

TURKS AND CAICOS ISLANDS (UK)
Area: 430sq km (166sq miles)
Population: 21,000
Capital: Cockburn Town

Cricket is a major sport in Jamaica. It was introduced by the British, who ruled the island for about 300 years until it became independent in 1962. The official language in Jamaica is English.

Little Abaco
Grand Bahama
Great Abaco
New Providence
Nassau
Andros

Gulf of Mexico
Havana
Matanzas
Pinar del Río
Santa Clara
Cienfuegos
Sancti Spiritus
Morón
Ciego de Avila
Isle of Youth
CUBA
Camagüey

BAHAMA

George Town
CAYMAN ISLANDS (UK)

Montego Bay
Kin
Spanish Tow
JAMAIC

Caribbean Sea

Sugar cane is grown in many Caribbean islands and it is Cuba's leading export. The islands also produce minerals, including nickel (Cuba), iron and nickel (Dominican Republic) and bauxite (Jamaica).

Banking and other financial services are important in the Bahamas. Many foreign firms and banks have branches there. The islands have no direct taxes and so many people invest money in the banks.

Tourism is a major activity in the Caribbean. Swimming and snorkelling in the sparkling, sunlit water around the islands in the Bahamas are popular sports. More than 1.5 million tourists visit the Bahamas every year.

Eleuthera

Cat

San Salvador

Rum Cay

Great Exuma

Long

Crooked

Mayaguana

Acklins

Great Inagua

• Holguín

Guantánamo

• Santiago de Cuba

Cockburn Town

TURKS AND CAICOS ISLANDS (UK)

ATLANTIC OCEAN

San Juan is the capital and largest city of Puerto Rico, a self-governing commonwealth in association with the United States. The chief jobs of the people are in manufacturing, trade and government.

Cap-Haïtien

Santiago

San Francisco

Gona'ves •

HAITI

DOMINICAN REPUBLIC

Port-au-Prince

La Romana

PUERTO RICO (US)

San Juan

Santo Domingo

Les Cayes

Jacmel

Ponce

| 0 | | 100 miles |
| 0 | | 100 kilometres |

Roman Catholicism was introduced into Cuba and the Dominican Republic by Spain, and into Haiti by France. But Protestantism is important in Jamaica and the Bahamas, which were influenced by Britain.

EASTERN CARIBBEAN

The eastern Caribbean consists mostly of small islands. Some are volcanic, while others are made of coral and limestone. The region contains eight independent countries and eight territories linked to France, the Netherlands, the United States and the UK. Farming and tourism are the chief activities, though Trinidad and Tobago has oil and natural gas. Native Americans once lived on the islands, but people of African descent now form the majority.

Dolphins of several species live in the waters of the Caribbean Sea. Tourists on cruise ships enjoy watching the dolphins. Fishing is an important industry, but nearly all of the catch is sold in local markets.

Tourism is a major industry in the eastern Caribbean.The islands are scenically beautiful and have many attractive, sun-baked beaches. Many people visit the islands on cruise ships.

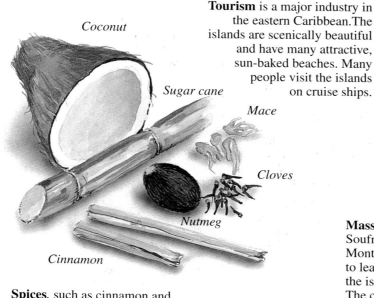

Coconut

Sugar cane

Mace

Cloves

Nutmeg

Cinnamon

Spices, such as cinnamon and nutmeg, are grown on some of the islands in the eastern Caribbean. The main products of the islands include bananas, coconuts, cotton and sugar.

Massive eruptions of the Soufrière Hills volcano, on Montserrat, forced many people to leave their homes or leave the island in the late 1990s. The capital Plymouth was covered by volcanic ash and is now deserted.

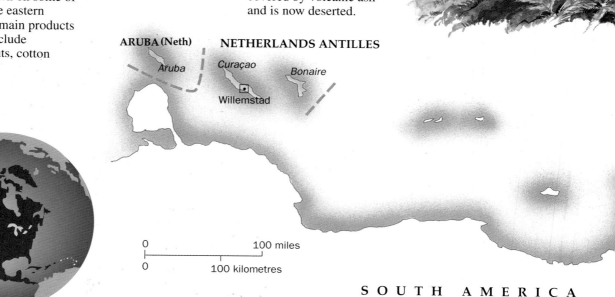

(UK)
Road Town
Charlotte Amalie
VIRGIN ISLAND
(US)

ARUBA (Neth)

NETHERLANDS ANTILLES

Aruba

Curaçao

Bonaire

Willemstad

0   100 miles

0   100 kilometres

SOUTH AMERICA

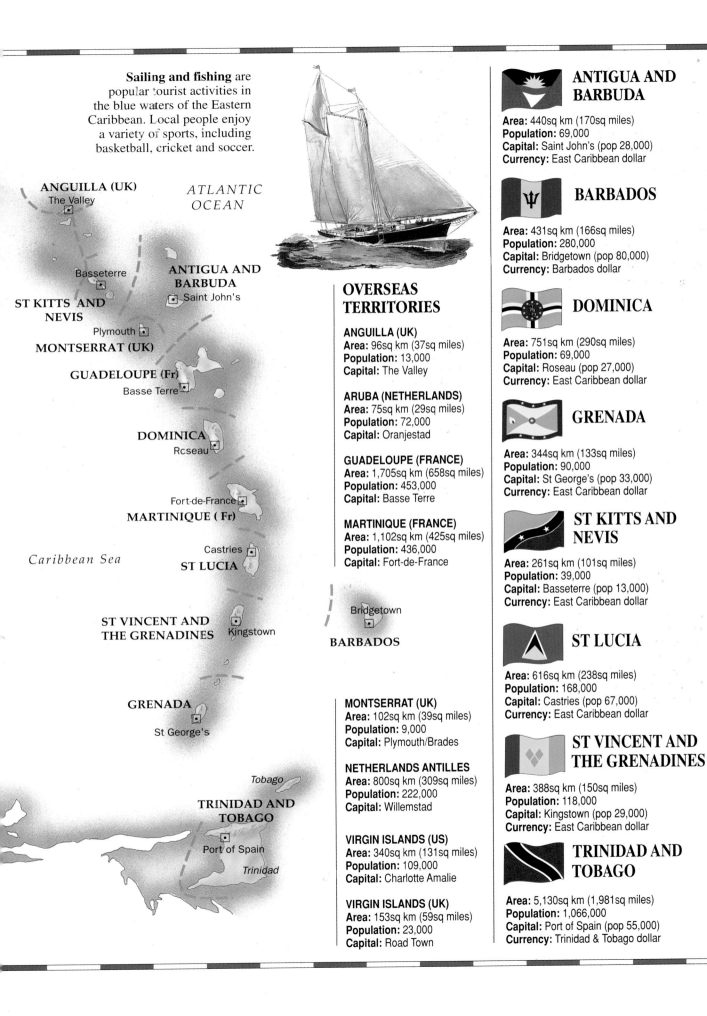

Sailing and fishing are popular tourist activities in the blue waters of the Eastern Caribbean. Local people enjoy a variety of sports, including basketball, cricket and soccer.

ATLANTIC OCEAN

ANGUILLA (UK)
The Valley

Basseterre

ST KITTS AND NEVIS

ANTIGUA AND BARBUDA
Saint John's

Plymouth

MONTSERRAT (UK)

GUADELOUPE (Fr)
Basse Terre

DOMINICA
Roseau

Fort-de-France

MARTINIQUE (Fr)

Caribbean Sea

Castries

ST LUCIA

ST VINCENT AND THE GRENADINES
Kingstown

Bridgetown

BARBADOS

GRENADA
St George's

Tobago

TRINIDAD AND TOBAGO
Port of Spain

Trinidad

OVERSEAS TERRITORIES

ANGUILLA (UK)
Area: 96sq km (37sq miles)
Population: 13,000
Capital: The Valley

ARUBA (NETHERLANDS)
Area: 75sq km (29sq miles)
Population: 72,000
Capital: Oranjestad

GUADELOUPE (FRANCE)
Area: 1,705sq km (658sq miles)
Population: 453,000
Capital: Basse Terre

MARTINIQUE (FRANCE)
Area: 1,102sq km (425sq miles)
Population: 436,000
Capital: Fort-de-France

MONTSERRAT (UK)
Area: 102sq km (39sq miles)
Population: 9,000
Capital: Plymouth/Brades

NETHERLANDS ANTILLES
Area: 800sq km (309sq miles)
Population: 222,000
Capital: Willemstad

VIRGIN ISLANDS (US)
Area: 340sq km (131sq miles)
Population: 109,000
Capital: Charlotte Amalie

VIRGIN ISLANDS (UK)
Area: 153sq km (59sq miles)
Population: 23,000
Capital: Road Town

ANTIGUA AND BARBUDA

Area: 440sq km (170sq miles)
Population: 69,000
Capital: Saint John's (pop 28,000)
Currency: East Caribbean dollar

BARBADOS

Area: 431sq km (166sq miles)
Population: 280,000
Capital: Bridgetown (pop 80,000)
Currency: Barbados dollar

DOMINICA

Area: 751sq km (290sq miles)
Population: 69,000
Capital: Roseau (pop 27,000)
Currency: East Caribbean dollar

GRENADA

Area: 344sq km (133sq miles)
Population: 90,000
Capital: St George's (pop 33,000)
Currency: East Caribbean dollar

ST KITTS AND NEVIS

Area: 261sq km (101sq miles)
Population: 39,000
Capital: Basseterre (pop 13,000)
Currency: East Caribbean dollar

ST LUCIA

Area: 616sq km (238sq miles)
Population: 168,000
Capital: Castries (pop 67,000)
Currency: East Caribbean dollar

ST VINCENT AND THE GRENADINES

Area: 388sq km (150sq miles)
Population: 118,000
Capital: Kingstown (pop 29,000)
Currency: East Caribbean dollar

TRINIDAD AND TOBAGO

Area: 5,130sq km (1,981sq miles)
Population: 1,066,000
Capital: Port of Spain (pop 55,000)
Currency: Trinidad & Tobago dollar

PEOPLE AND BELIEFS

North America contains eight per cent of the world's population. Vast areas, including most of Canada and Alaska and the deserts of the southwestern United States and northern Mexico, are almost empty of people. Thickly populated areas, with many huge cities, occur in the eastern United States, California, the Mexican plateau, Central America and the Caribbean.

Population densities in North America

Number of people per square kilometre

- Over 100
- Between 50 and 100
- Between 10 and 50
- Between 1 and 10
- Below 1

The main cities

- Cities of more than 1,000,000 people
- Cities of more than 500,000 people

Population and area

Although Canada is the world's second largest country, its population of over 30 million is only about one-ninth that of the United States and one-third that of Mexico. Around 200 years ago, more than 90 per cent of North Americans lived in rural areas and farmed the land. Today 65 per cent live in towns and cities, including Mexico City, the continent's largest, New York City, Los Angeles and Chicago.

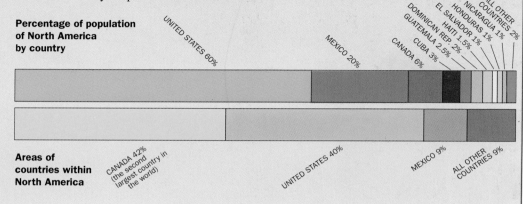

Percentage of population of North America by country

UNITED STATES 60%
MEXICO 20%
CANADA 6%
CUBA 3%
GUATEMALA 2.5%
DOMINICAN REP. 2%
EL SALVADOR 1%
HAITI 1.5%
HONDURAS 1%
NICARAGUA 1%
ALL OTHER COUNTRIES 2%

Areas of countries within North America

CANADA 42% (the second largest country in the world)
UNITED STATES 40%
MEXICO 9%
ALL OTHER COUNTRIES 9%

Main religions

Early French settlers introduced Roman Catholicism into Canada and today Roman Catholics make up 43 per cent of the population. Protestants make up 52 per cent of the population of the United States and Roman Catholics 24 per cent.

Roman Catholicism dominates the Latin American countries to the south, though traces of ancient Native American religions are sometimes evident in church rituals. Voodoo, which is practised in Haiti, combines elements of African religions and Christianity.

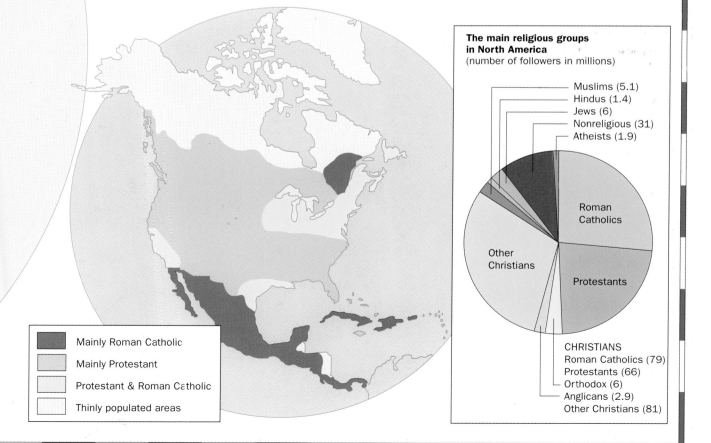

Mainly Roman Catholic
Mainly Protestant
Protestant & Roman Catholic
Thinly populated areas

The main religious groups in North America
(number of followers in millions)

Muslims (5.1)
Hindus (1.4)
Jews (6)
Nonreligious (31)
Atheists (1.9)

Roman Catholics
Other Christians
Protestants

CHRISTIANS
Roman Catholics (79)
Protestants (66)
Orthodox (6)
Anglicans (2.9)
Other Christians (81)

CLIMATE AND VEGETATION

North America has every kind of climatic and vegetation region. The north is cold, but the United States has large areas of temperate forest and grasslands. Deserts cover parts of the southwestern United States, while southern Mexico, the Caribbean and Central America lie in the hot tropics.

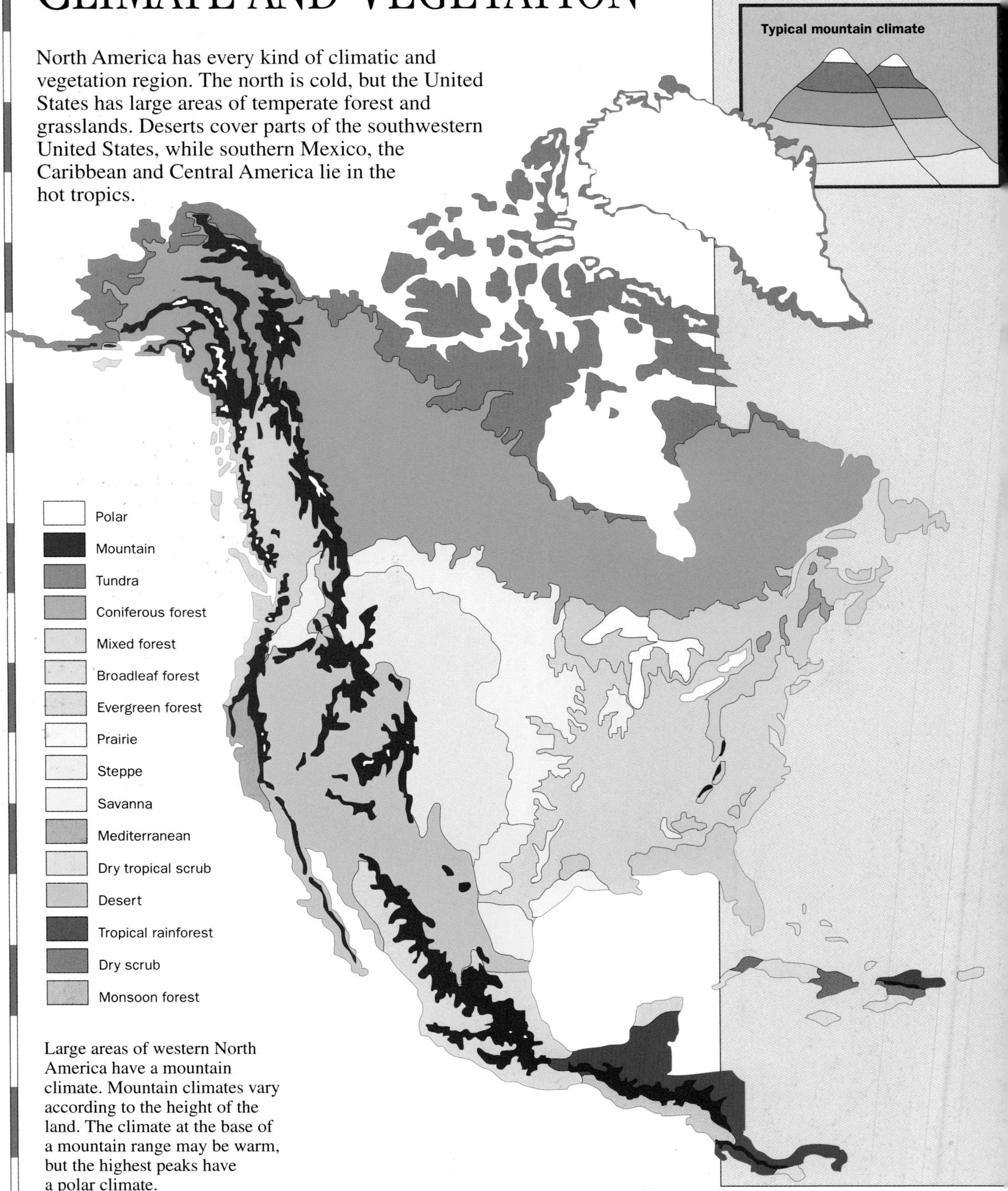

Typical mountain climate

Polar
Mountain
Tundra
Coniferous forest
Mixed forest
Broadleaf forest
Evergreen forest
Prairie
Steppe
Savanna
Mediterranean
Dry tropical scrub
Desert
Tropical rainforest
Dry scrub
Monsoon forest

Large areas of western North America have a mountain climate. Mountain climates vary according to the height of the land. The climate at the base of a mountain range may be warm, but the highest peaks have a polar climate.

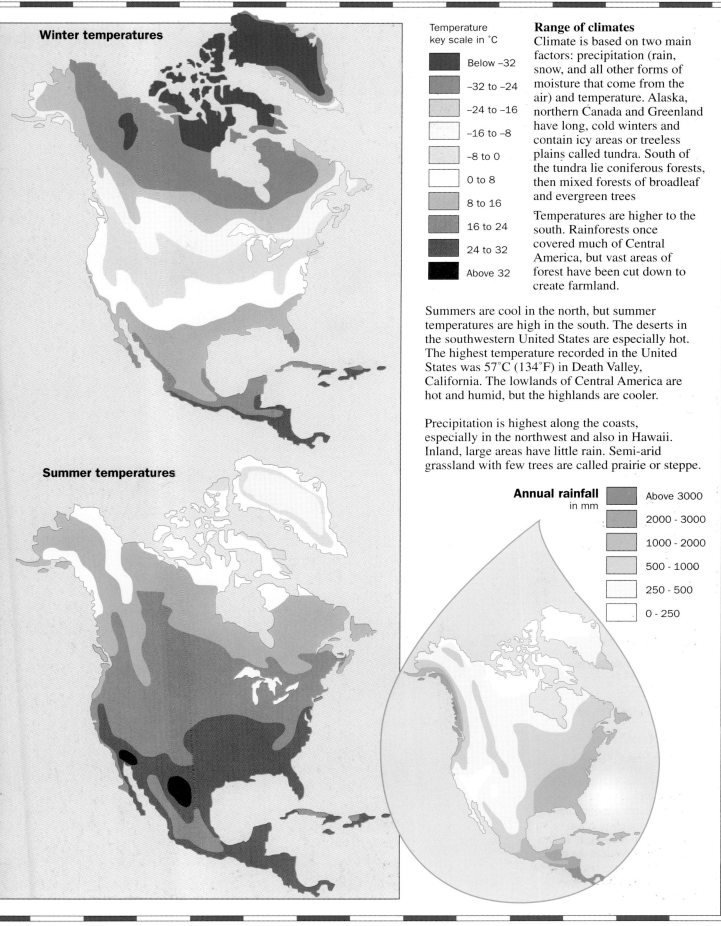

Winter temperatures

Summer temperatures

Temperature
key scale in °C

	Below –32
	–32 to –24
	–24 to –16
	–16 to –8
	–8 to 0
	0 to 8
	8 to 16
	16 to 24
	24 to 32
	Above 32

Range of climates

Climate is based on two main factors: precipitation (rain, snow, and all other forms of moisture that come from the air) and temperature. Alaska, northern Canada and Greenland have long, cold winters and contain icy areas or treeless plains called tundra. South of the tundra lie coniferous forests, then mixed forests of broadleaf and evergreen trees

Temperatures are higher to the south. Rainforests once covered much of Central America, but vast areas of forest have been cut down to create farmland.

Summers are cool in the north, but summer temperatures are high in the south. The deserts in the southwestern United States are especially hot. The highest temperature recorded in the United States was 57°C (134°F) in Death Valley, California. The lowlands of Central America are hot and humid, but the highlands are cooler.

Precipitation is highest along the coasts, especially in the northwest and also in Hawaii. Inland, large areas have little rain. Semi-arid grassland with few trees are called prairie or steppe.

Annual rainfall
in mm

	Above 3000
	2000 - 3000
	1000 - 2000
	500 - 1000
	250 - 500
	0 - 250

ECOLOGY AND ENVIRONMENT

The land is always changing. Natural forces, such as volcanic eruptions, great storms and unceasing erosion contribute to the change. People also change the land. Human activities cause pollution, while intensive farming exposes the land to the wind and rain, turning former grasslands into desert.

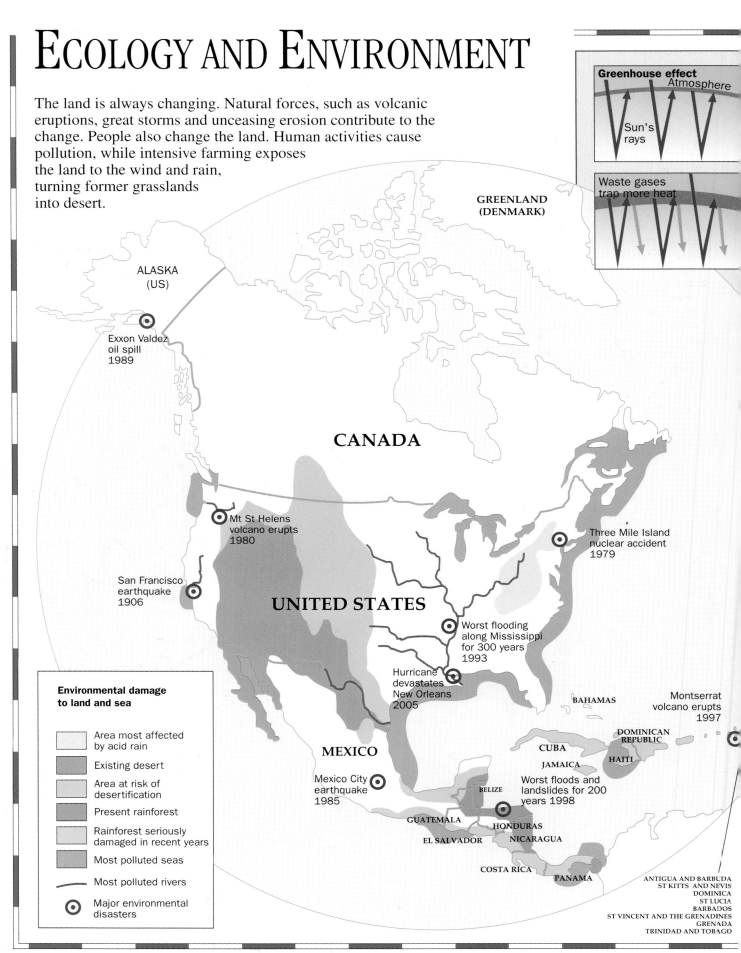

Greenhouse effect
Atmosphere

Sun's rays

Waste gases trap more heat

GREENLAND (DENMARK)

ALASKA (US)

Exxon Valdez oil spill 1989

CANADA

Mt St Helens volcano erupts 1980

Three Mile Island nuclear accident 1979

San Francisco earthquake 1906

UNITED STATES

Worst flooding along Mississippi for 300 years 1993

Hurricane devastates New Orleans 2005

BAHAMAS

Montserrat volcano erupts 1997

DOMINICAN REPUBLIC

MEXICO

CUBA

JAMAICA

HAITI

Mexico City earthquake 1985

BELIZE

Worst floods and landslides for 200 years 1998

GUATEMALA

HONDURAS

EL SALVADOR

NICARAGUA

COSTA RICA

PANAMA

ANTIGUA AND BARBUDA
ST KITTS AND NEVIS
DOMINICA
ST LUCIA
BARBADOS
ST VINCENT AND THE GRENADINES
GRENADA
TRINIDAD AND TOBAGO

Environmental damage to land and sea

- Area most affected by acid rain
- Existing desert
- Area at risk of desertification
- Present rainforest
- Rainforest seriously damaged in recent years
- Most polluted seas
- Most polluted rivers
- Major environmental disasters

Damaging the environment

Air pollution is a problem in North America where factories, cars and homes emit waste gases into the air. Some gases dissolve in water vapour and cause acid rain which kills trees. Excess carbon dioxide increases the atmosphere's natural greenhouse effect and may be causing global warming.

The clearing of forests and of grasslands lays soil bare. Strong winds and rain remove the topsoil making the land barren. The destruction of rainforests also threatens many living creatures with extinction.

Water pollution is caused by agricultural chemicals and waste from factories being washed or pumped into rivers and lakes, and by oil spills and untreated sewage at sea. Pollution is also caused by accidents at nuclear power stations. Today, people are working to combat pollution and its deadly effects.

Natural hazards

Earthquakes are common in western North America and the Caribbean, which lie on unstable parts of the earth's crust. Volcanic eruptions occur in Alaska, Washington, Mexico, Central America and the Caribbean. Hurricanes cause great damage in the Caribbean and the southeastern United States, while violent tornadoes tear through the central plains of the United States. Devastating floods occur when rivers overflow.

Natural hazards

Earthquake zones

▲ Active volcanoes

Hurricane tracks (June to October)

Tornado danger areas

Endangered species

North America was once a vast, mostly empty, wilderness, where many wild animals flourished. But in the last 400 years, hunting and the destruction of natural vegetation have greatly reduced the numbers of animals. Some species are close to extinction.

Fortunately, many endangered species are now protected and some have begun to recover their numbers. Even the bald eagle, symbol of the United States, was threatened, but the US government announced in 2007 that its numbers had recovered sufficiently for it to be removed from the endangered list after 40 years. The ivory-billed woodpecker, thought to be extinct, was rediscovered in 2004.

California condor

Some endangered species of North America

Birds
California condor
Eskimo curlew
Ivory-billed woodpecker

Mammals
Black bear
Black-footed ferret
Central American tapir
Jaguarundi
Polar bear
Volcano rabbit

Marine animals
Grey whale
Leatherback turtle
Manatee

Trees
Caribbean mahogany
Giant sequoia

ECONOMY

North America is rich in natural resources, including coal, oil,
gas and most of the metals used in industry. It also has forests
and large areas of fertile farmland. The most developed
countries are the United States and Canada. Together,
they produce about one-third of the world's
industrial goods.

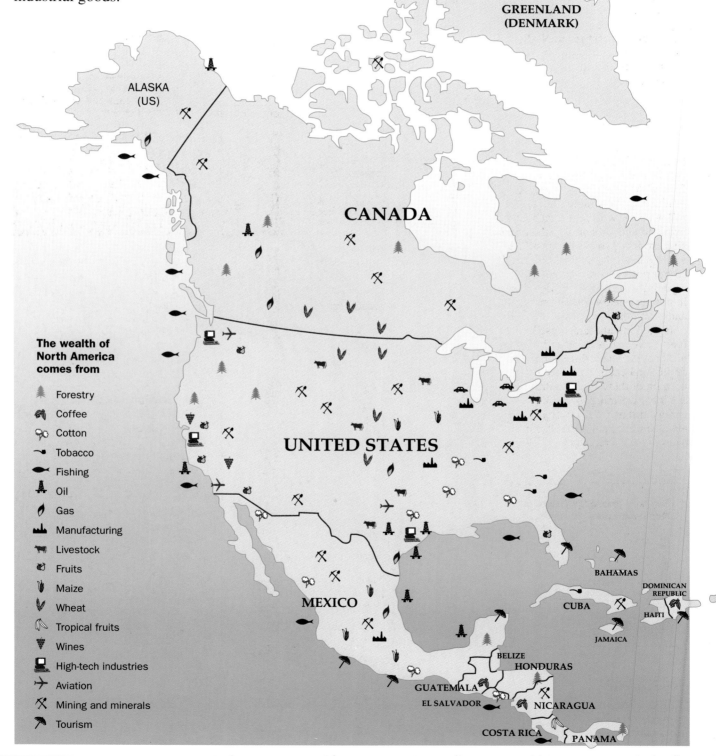

**GREENLAND
(DENMARK)**

ALASKA
(US)

CANADA

**The wealth of
North America
comes from**

🌲 Forestry

🍇 Coffee

🌿 Cotton

🌰 Tobacco

🐟 Fishing

🛢 Oil

🍃 Gas

🏭 Manufacturing

🐄 Livestock

🍎 Fruits

🌽 Maize

🌾 Wheat

🍌 Tropical fruits

🍷 Wines

💻 High-tech industries

✈ Aviation

⚒ Mining and minerals

🌂 Tourism

UNITED STATES

MEXICO

BAHAMAS

DOMINICAN
REPUBLIC

CUBA

HAITI

JAMAICA

BELIZE

HONDURAS

GUATEMALA

EL SALVADOR

NICARAGUA

COSTA RICA

PANAMA

Gross domestic product

In order to compare the economies of countries, experts work out the gross domestic product (GDP) of the countries in US dollars. The GDP is the total value of all the goods and services produced in a country in a year. The chart, right, shows that the GDP of the United States is more than seven times bigger than the combined GDP of all the other countries in North America. No country in the world has a higher GDP than the United States.

GDP for the countries of North America
(in billions of dollars)

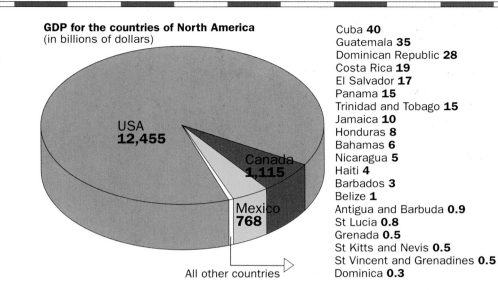

USA **12,455**

Canada **1,115**

Mexico **768**

All other countries

Cuba **40**
Guatemala **35**
Dominican Republic **28**
Costa Rica **19**
El Salvador **17**
Panama **15**
Trinidad and Tobago **15**
Jamaica **10**
Honduras **8**
Bahamas **6**
Nicaragua **5**
Haiti **4**
Barbados **3**
Belize **1**
Antigua and Barbuda **0.9**
St Lucia **0.8**
Grenada **0.5**
St Kitts and Nevis **0.5**
St Vincent and Grenadines **0.5**
Dominica **0.3**

Per capita GDPs
Per capita means per head or per person. Per capita GDPs are worked out by dividing the GDP by the population. For example, the per capita GDP of the United States is $41,700. Canada has a per capita GDP of $33,700. Haiti has a per capita GDP of only $510.

Sources of energy

North America produces about a fifth of the world's oil. The leading producer is the United States, followed by Mexico, Canada, and Trinidad and Tobago. North America also produces about a third of the world's natural gas. Hydroelectricity (water power) is important, especially in Canada, while other important energy sources are coal and uranium.

In the United States, fossil fuels (coal, natural gas and oil) provide about three-quarters of the total energy produced. The burning of these fuels contributes to global warming. Nuclear energy and hydroelectricity are also important. Renewable sources are increasing.

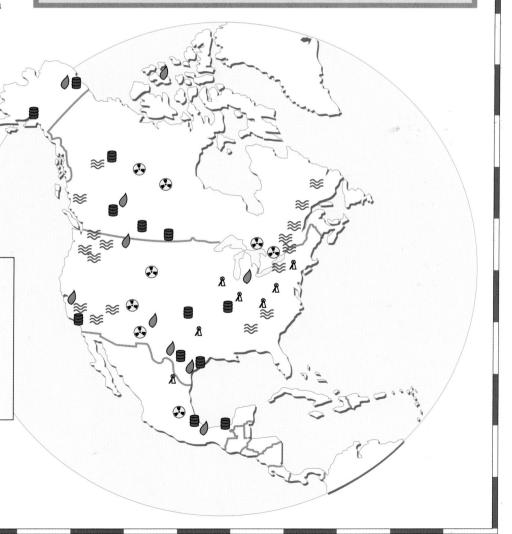

Sources of energy found in North America

- 🛢 Oil
- 💧 Gas
- ≋ Hydroelectricity
- ⚒ Coal
- ☢ Uranium

ANTIGUA AND BARBUDA
ST KITTS AND NEVIS
DOMINICA
ST LUCIA
BARBADOS
ST VINCENT AND THE GRENADINES
GRENADA
TRINIDAD AND TOBAGO

POLITICS AND HISTORY

North America contains 23 independent countries. The United States and Mexico are federal republics. Canada, Belize and eight Caribbean nations are constitutional monarchies. They have their own governments, but they recognize the British monarch as their head of state. Ten countries are democratic republics, while Cuba is a Communist republic. North America also includes 14 overseas territories linked to Britain, Denmark, France, Netherlands and the United States.

Longboats like these were used by the Vikings to explore the coasts of Greenland and mainland North America a thousand years ago

GREENLAND
(DENMARK)

ALASKA
(US)

CANADA

UNITED STATES

Great events
The timeline below begins with the arrival of the first people from Asia towards the end of the Great Ice Age. They were the ancestors of the Native Americans.

The modern history of North America began in 1492, when the explorer Christopher Columbus, sailing from Spain, reached the Caribbean Sea. He thought he had reached Asia, but instead he had found a 'New World' unknown to Europeans at that time. Following this discovery, many immigrants settled in North America. The United States declared its independence from Britain in 1776 and subsequently became the most powerful nation on earth.

Today the continent is populated by Native Americans and also by people of European, African and Asian origin.

Political system

	Federal republic
	Constitutional monarchy
	Democratic republic
	Communist republic
	Overseas territory

BAHAMAS

DOMINIC
REPUBLI

CUBA

HAITI

JAMAICA

MEXICO

BELIZE

HONDURAS

GUATEMALA

NICARAGUA

EL SALVADOR

COSTA RICA

PANAMA

Important dates

Early people cross from Asia and move south through North America

3000 Pottery being produced in what is now Mexico

1150 Olmec civilization founded in Mexico

550 Mesa Verde in Colorado, USA, built by Pueblo Indians

800 Mayan civilization founded in Central America

1000 Vikings from Greenland reach mainland of North America

1325 Rise of Aztecs in Mexico and the city of Tenochtitlán founded. It later became Mexico City

1492 Christopher Columbus reached 'New World'

1493 First Spanish settlers arrived in North America

1497 John Cabot voyaged to North America from England

1510 First African taken to A

| 10,000 BC | AD1 | AD1000 | 1500 |

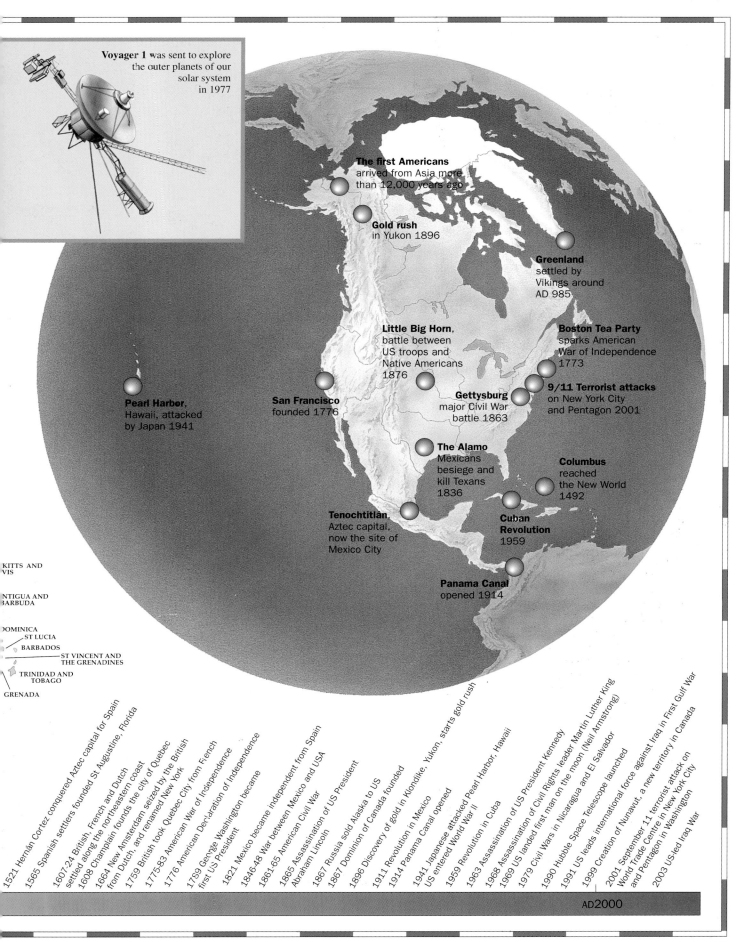

Voyager 1 was sent to explore the outer planets of our solar system in 1977

The first Americans arrived from Asia more than 12,000 years ago

Gold rush in Yukon 1896

Greenland settled by Vikings around AD 985

Little Big Horn, battle between US troops and Native Americans 1876

Boston Tea Party sparks American War of Independence 1773

9/11 Terrorist attacks on New York City and Pentagon 2001

San Francisco founded 1776

Gettysburg major Civil War battle 1863

Pearl Harbor, Hawaii, attacked by Japan 1941

The Alamo Mexicans besiege and kill Texans 1836

Columbus reached the New World 1492

Tenochtitlán, Aztec capital, now the site of Mexico City

Cuban Revolution 1959

Panama Canal opened 1914

KITTS AND
VIS

NTIGUA AND
BARBUDA

DOMINICA
ST LUCIA
BARBADOS
ST VINCENT AND
THE GRENADINES
TRINIDAD AND
TOBAGO
GRENADA

1521 Hernán Cortez conquered Aztec capital for Spain

1565 Spanish settlers founded St Augustine, Florida

1607-24 British, French and Dutch settled along the northeastern coast

1608 Champlain founds the city of Quebec

1664 New Amsterdam seized by the British from Dutch, and renamed New York

1759 British took Quebec City from French

1775-83 American War of Independence

1776 American Declaration of Independence

1789 George Washington became first US President

1821 Mexico became independent from Spain

1846-48 War between Mexico and USA

1861-65 American Civil War

1865 Assassination of US President Abraham Lincoln

1867 Russia sold Alaska to US

1867 Dominion of Canada founded

1896 Discovery of gold in Klondike, Yukon, starts gold rush

1911 Revolution in Mexico

1914 Panama Canal opened

1941 Japanese attacked Pearl Harbor, Hawaii US entered World War II

1959 Revolution in Cuba

1963 Assassination of US President Kennedy

1968 Assassination of Civil Rights leader Martin Luther King

1969 US landed first man on the moon (Neil Armstrong)

1979 Civil Wars in Nicaragua and El Salvador

1990 Hubble Space Telescope launched

1991 US leads international force against Iraq in First Gulf War

1999 Creation of Nunavut, a new territory in Canada

2001 September 11 terrorist attack on World Trade Centre in New York City and Pentagon in Washington

2003 US-led Iraq War

AD2000

INDEX

Picture credits
Photographs: Travel Photo International 1, 5, 9, 13, 21, 23, 25, 26, 27, 33, 34
AS Publishing 4, 10, 15
Keith Lye 4, 29